HOW TO
MAKE A
GARDEN GROW

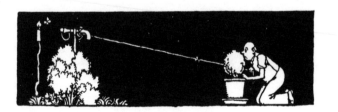

Crazy pavement for the roof garden

HOW TO
MAKE A
GARDEN GROW

By

HEATH ROBINSON
and

K. R. G. BROWNE

This edition first published in 2016 by the Bodleian Library
Broad Street
Oxford OX1 3BG

www.bodleianshop.co.uk

ISBN: 978 1 85124 4553

First published in 1938 by Hutchinson & Co. Ltd.

Cover design by Dot Little at the Bodleian Library
Designed and typeset by Roderick Teasdale in
11.5pt on 11.5pt Tw Cen MT Light
Printed and bound on 90gsm munken cream by
TJ International Ltd., Padstow, Cornwall

British Library Catalogue in Publishing Data
A CIP record of this publication is available from the British Library

Curing night starvation

A Refresher in the Bird Bath

CONTENTS

DEDICATION I

To young gardeners, old gardeners, gardeners in their second or third childhoods, bow-legged gardeners, gardeners bald, gardeners hirsute, gardeners in kilts, Kent or the kinematograph trade, strabismic or teetotal gardeners, gardeners on their honeymoon, gardeners named Popjoy or Snafflethwaite, gardeners who believe that the earth is flat, scorbutic gardeners, gardeners whose forebears came over with William the Conqueror, gardeners with double-jointed thumbs, gardeners whose forebears came over with a day-trip from the Isle of Man, gardeners who only do it for their health's sake, and gardeners not specifically referred to above—this book is dedicated with all possible respect and sympathy.

DEDICATION II

And the same applies to all who live by, for or on behalf of gardens, viz: florists' apprentices, tulip-importers, the Royal Horticultural Society, wholesale seedsmen of all sizes, trowel-testers, clothes-peg manufacturers, rockery-architects, buttonhole-cutters, hammock-salesmen, and even jobbing-gardeners with waterfall moustaches.

Two Dedications for the price of one! What more could the heart desire?

Mistake at a garden party

INTRODUCTION

It was Napoleon, I believe, who once remarked laughingly across the teacups to somebody whose name escapes me for the moment: "These English (ces anglais et anglaises) are a nation of gardeners! *Zut, alors!*"

Rather a sweeping statement, but one containing more than a grain of truth. Horticulture does not, of course, play so large a part in Great Britain's daily life as professional football or the bacon-curing industry; but of every ten Englishmen accosted at random in the street—somewhat to their surprise, no doubt—at least six would prove to be keen amateurs of the trowel, the shears and the twopenny seed-packet. (The other four would probably start nervously and hurry on, suspecting a catch somewhere.)

HOW TO MAKE A GARDEN GROW

Affection for flowers of all sorts has been a British characteristic since the dawn of Time. In their earliest forms, presumably, gardens were merely bits of ground on which things either grew or did not. It is likely, indeed, that the Early British caveholder never even realized that he *had* a garden until flowers actually sprouted on his premises. Knowing nothing of the gardener's art, he had to take what Nature chose to give him in the way of flora; but as he was unable to distinguish an orchid from a dandelion—and, in any case, was far too busy keeping the megatherium from the door—that worried him very little, one imagines.

Nowadays, however, gardening is a highly complicated science, bristling with Latin phrases and giving employment to a large number of deserving workers. The manufacturers of hose-pipery, the designers of garden-rollers, the intrepid experts who insert the essential teeth in rakes, the knitters of netting for nut-trees, the elderly ladies who purvey rich blooms from baskets at street-corners, the distillers of insecticide, the skilled craftsmen who operate

Affection for flowers

the interlocutory bivalvular Hoppskotsch machines which impart the essential rotundity to the ball-bearings of lawn-mowers—all these, and many more, owe their livelihood and an occasional egg with their tea to the unknown genius who first discovered that flowers can be made (or, at any rate, encouraged) to bloom in the Spring, tra la!

10

INTRODUCTION

What nature gave him

Not everybody, admittedly, can cultivate the type of garden that gets its photograph in the glossier weekly papers and is visited by charabanc-loads of awestruck sightseers during the geranium season. Almost anybody, however, who owns the first British serial rights in a plot of ground, a pair of old trousers, a philosophic disposition and a little spare cash—wherewith to buy fertilizer, wallflower-bulbs, gardening-gloves and embrocation (for aches in the back, without which no gardener can properly discharge his duties)—can devise a modest pleasaunce in which tea can be taken on summer afternoons and which can be boasted about slightly at the Club.

Though a lot of Britons now inhabit flats—and many of them pretty comfortably, too, thanks to Mr. Heath Robinson and myself (advt.)—the bulk of the

Many have not seen their feet for years

population still prefers to live in houses, each with its allotted ration of this blessed plot, this earth, this realm, this England. This is all to the good, in the opinion of authorities on hygiene, because even the smallest garden is a good place to get fresh air and gentle exercise in. The larger the garden, of course, the less gentle the exercise; but quite a lot of healthful stooping can be done in the most restricted of back-yards.

(There is an old Chinese adage to the effect that indifferent stoopers make bad gardeners; but this is only partly true. People who, by reason of their age and/or physical contours, stoop slowly and with reluctance will naturally not get such quick results as those who bend featly and without discomfort; and, obviously, they will require stouter braces. But to regard gardening, on that account, as a pastime solely for the young and lissome is to turn a blind ear to the evidence. Some of the finest gardeners in History were practically circular, while many of those at large today have not seen their feet for years.)

Nor, in order to enjoy a garden, is it necessary to be on intimate terms with every variety of flower. To the eye of a true beauty-lover a humble patch of that hardy perennial, old-maid's-bedsock, is just as pleasing as a bed of the rare and costly *psittacosis pennsylvania*, which blooms only on the 29th of February in alternate Leap Years. The rarest flowers are often the most hideous, and the amateur need not be ashamed to work on the common (or garden) assorted-seed-packet system, rather than despatch emissaries to the far corners of the globe in search of exotic plants.

That gardening is good for the soul will be denied by nobody who has ever tried it. Only those who have ministered to an ailing peony or sat up all night with a sick chrysanthemum know how such experiences enrich

A sick chrysanthemum

*Self-elevator to be used when
thinning hot-house grapes*

the mind and stimulate the thought-processes. The first snowdrop, timidly thrusting its rather silly head through the earth's crust, is a sight to melt the heart of the toughest thug that ever throttled his aged grandmother for her insurance-money. To watch a tulip grow from innocent bulbhood to full maturity without the slightest assistance from the Government is to realize that the ways of Nature, mysterious though they be, are at least preferable to those of Mr.——, the well-known company-promoter.

In other words, a garden is a lovesome thing, God wot! Realizing this (so quick are we on the uptake), Mr. Heath Robinson and I have designed this modest but not unattractive work, a copy of which should be placed immediately in every potting-shed.

We need hardly say that months of research and experiment have gone to the making of this book. Although Mr. Heath Robinson's window-box is a by-word in the neighbourhood, while I can easily distinguish the scent of violets from that of a glue-factory, we have not hitherto been known as really first-class gardeners. In fact, when we first embarked upon this enterprise, a primrose by the river's brim a simple cowslip was to us, and it was nothing more; while when we called a spade a spade, we did so hesitantly, wondering if it ought not to be called a shovel.

Things are jolly different now, however. It is not for us to blow our own clarinets, so I will not detail the methods, mostly rather shady, by which we acquired the mass of gardening lore which is set forth in these pages. It is enough to say that no expense has been spared, and no hardship shirked, in our efforts to

Shady methods of acquiring gardening lore

compile a comprehensive textbook for the guidance of those who yearn to make two orchids grow where only plantains grew before.

That, anyway, is our story; and we mean to stick to it. And if, as a result of our labours, next year's rose-crop is not considerably above the average, we shall be forced to the conclusion that something has gone wrong somewhere.

Curling curly-kale

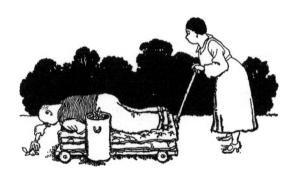

To Save Stooping

LAYING OUT THE GARDEN

From the novice horticulturist's point of view, there are only two kinds of garden. There is (a) the untilled patch of virgin soil, rich in sardine-tins and old boots, which is found at the back of brand-new houses; and there is (b) the already matured garden, developed by a previous tenant who has just left the neighbourhood, either to visit relatives in Khamschatka or to sojourn awhile in gaol.

If the beginner's garden is of the latter sort, he will probably feel too shy to meddle with it until he has thoroughly digested his "Gardening Hints" series of cigarette-cards and taken a few digging-lessons. Eventually, no doubt, he will decide to reorganize it somewhat; but for the time being he is content to know that it is more or less growing itself.

This chapter, therefore, is addressed chiefly to

An Interesting Layout for a Small Pleasure Garden

those whose garden, at the moment of going to press, is just a naked piece of Mother Earth, flowerless as the Mojave Desert and clamouring to be given a start in life—or "laid out", as it is technically termed.

In laying out a garden, the first point to decide is whether it shall be purely ornamental (i.e. flowers, etc.), definitely useful (i.e. veg. and the like), or a bit of each. In this matter the beginner must follow the dictates of his heart, always remembering that much depends on the space at his disposal, and even more on the opinions of his wife.

In this day and age, when open-air exercise is so popular with all classes of Society, many householders regard a tennis-court as an essential feature of a garden; others, of a more lethargic temperament, feel the same about a croquet-lawn. In homes where the husband is a tennis-fan and the wife a croquet-addict, it is usually advisable to compromise and have a croquet-lawn; but those who are opposed to this course are respectfully urged to study the accompanying diagram, which shows that it is possible, by the exercise of a little ingenuity, to accommodate a tennis-court, a croquet-lawn, a bowling-green and even a golf-course in a garden that would cramp the style of a professional cat-swinger. After all, tennis on slightly reduced terms is just as enjoyable as the full-sized variety—more so, indeed, for players of advanced years who suffer from fallen arches. As for croquet, many golfers hold that the less there is of it, the better; and the same applies to golf from the croquet-player's viewpoint.

It is impossible, however—or uncomfortable, anyway—to play either tennis or croquet on an uneven surface. In other words, the ground must be carefully

Levelling the Lawn

levelled before the local clergy are invited to pop on their sandshoes and play on it, as there is no more embarrassing guest than a Vicar who has stubbed his toe against a mole-hill or sprained his ankle in a rabbit-hole while attempting to put over a fast one.

The best method of levelling lawns, of course, is to employ professional lawn-levellers, who can be chartered by the day, week or month and give very little trouble about the house; but quite good results can be obtained with the help of an upright piano, a couple of rather obese relatives, a borrowed motorcar and some stout rope. As the illustration shows, the piano is laid on the ground and the relatives on the piano, which is then attached by the rope to the car and towed briskly back and forth. Gardeners whose relatives are on a diet and therefore too light for this purpose, will find that the addition of two bestselling eight-and-sixpenny novels dealing with the amatory permutations of a Middle Western family will usually do the trick.

For those who are too old for tennis, too young for croquet, too sensible for golf and too rich for mere vegetable-culture, Mr. Heath Robinson has designed (see diagram), a very natty little garden of the purely ornamental type—or "Stonemason's Joy", as it is termed in the trade.

Gardens of this kind are intended to be walked round and looked at, rather than romped in and dug up; and there is no doubt that they make a pretty big impression on the neighbours. Top hats can be worn in them with impunity, and birds below the rank of eagle seldom venture within their boundaries. Moreover, they are quite inexpensive to maintain, the masonry needing only an occasional rub with a duster and the goldfish their daily meed of ants' eggs to keep them in the pink.

Testing the Level of a New Lawn

In the example illustrated, the Greek columns supporting the hammock are a particularly happy touch, as they emphasize the slightly formal note characteristic of such gardens, and enable the hammock-dweller to strike matches with the minimum of effort. The bird-bath in the foreground is fitted with h. & c. and is the latest thing from Paris; while those who object on moral grounds to nudity in fishpond-statuary can always have the latter fitted with a little waterproof bodice.

The fountain is by permission of the Metropolitan Water Board; but some gardeners are so fortunate as to have on their premises a natural spring which can be employed for this purpose. Gardeners who have a natural spring but no craving for a fountain—for, when all is said, there is no accounting for tastes—can divert the former into the next garden in the manner shown, thereby avoiding the risk of floods in the herbaceous border and giving the man next door considerable food for thought.

Diverting an Unwanted Spring

Artistic Layout for a Purely Ornamental Garden

*Careful Preparation of the Soil Before Planting
a Rose-Bed*

It is doubtful, however, if the formal type of garden will appeal to the majority of beginners. The novice's natural instinct is neither to play tennis nor to gape at statues, but to grow things—artichokes, antirrhinums, or whatever it may be—at once and in large quantities.

It should be borne in mind, therefore, that few plants will sprout successfully on an unprepared foundation. It is useless, for example, to hurl sunflower-bulbs at random into a meadow and expect them to bear fruit, while rose-seeds dropped casually on a piece of earth rarely produce anything worth looking at. If it is to give the best results, ground must be thoroughly vetted, manicured and otherwise got ready before anything is planted in it. Even then there is no certainty that anything will come up; but the gardener can at least feel that he has done his best and can reasonably blame the weather (or the political crisis in Peru, or the fact that the 5.15 from Basingstoke does not stop at Hull) for his failure to produce anything larger than a small forget-me-not.

One of the first tasks, then, confronting the beginner is that of overhauling his soil, which he will find, in all probability, simply bristling with large stones, long-defunct cats, disused salmon-tins, worms, more large stones, Roman pottery, and similar bric-a-brac. The worms may be left to work out their own salvation; the ex-cats and salmon-tins can be thrown

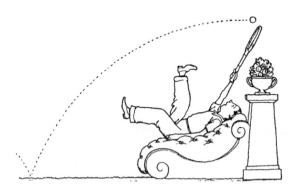

Artistic Terminal to the Run-Back of a Tennis Court

25

A Simple Method of Removing Stones

over the fence under cover of darkness; the Roman pottery will be welcomed by any local museum; and the stones can be assembled and removed (as shown) with the help of an agile assistant, an ordinary sieve and a commodious shovel.

Testing the Rate of Drainage in a Garden Path

LAYING OUT THE GARDEN

Paths are more or less essential, too, a pathless garden being not only a contradiction in terms but highly inconvenient, as anybody will agree who has ever had to hop across a cabbage-patch in order to inspect a pedigree lobelia. Unlike the road to Hell, garden-paths are normally surfaced with gravel, which can be obtained gratis from any convenient gravel-pit when nobody is looking, and distributed where required by means of the Heath Robinson Perambeller, or Gravulator, which is here depicted.

The foregoing, we trust, will help the hesitant beginner both to choose the type of garden best suited to his needs, and to get it vaguely organized for planting. If he is decided on these points, and has not suddenly resolved to give up gardening altogether and go in for art-needlework instead, we must ask him to turn this page (*without* moistening the thumb and forefinger), and get another earful.

But, frankly, if he would rather go to the pictures, it is perfectly O.K. with us.

To Ensure an Even Distribution of Gravel

27

Window-Box Greenhouse for Those without a Garden

A Well-Trained Tree

PLANTS AND FLOWERS

Having planned his garden, more or less prepared the ground, and ironed out the resultant knots in his delving-muscles, the gardener is faced with the problem of deciding what to plant, and where, and even why. His first step should be to select a few trees and shrubs, as these will temper the wind to the shorn violet in inclement weather, while on summer afternoons their shade is very pleasant to recline in with a good book. Washing can also be hung out on them, if it is that kind of neighbourhood.

In the matter of trees, the beginner would do well to remember that the larger varieties, such as the oak,

29

Thoughtfully Pruned Trees

the elm, the poplar and the *aesculus hippocastanum*—or "the horse-chestnut", as it is sometimes called to distinguish it from the chestnut horse, which is a very different thing—are not quick sprouters. Though an oak-tree adds a touch of dignity to any garden, it develops so slowly that long before it is really grownup its original owner has handed in his dinner-pail and become a faint but fragrant memory to his relations.

The beginner, therefore, is advised to plant only those smaller tree-shrubs, or shrub-trees, which are guaranteed to bear fruit, if any, in his lifetime. In choosing these he need not be deterred by their extensive Latin names—many of which can be set to music and sung at ships' concerts without fee—as these are only added to make it more difficult and usually mean something quite simple, such as a gum-tree. *Polygala chamaebuxus*, for example (which is often mistaken by novices for a Caucasian potentate or a disease of the inner ear), is only six inches tall and can easily be carried in one hand. *Ulex*, again, is not—as some people suppose—a patent remedy for digestive disorders, but merely a gorse-bush.

Many of the more popular shrubs, notably the rhododendron, the magnolia and the hydrangea, scorn to employ an alias and so can be ordered fearlessly by anybody who can spell or pronounce them. It is to this group that Miss Sadie Doolittle Sapp, "the Shenectady Songbird", refers, rather ambiguously, in her "Collected Poems, or The Darkling Egg":

"Though the Texas Rangers
Know very little about hydrangeas,
Unlike the majority of British actors,
They know a lot about cactus."

(Taking no chances, however, Mr. Heath Robinson has designed, for the benefit of those British actors who are cactus-conscious, a handy de-spiking machine

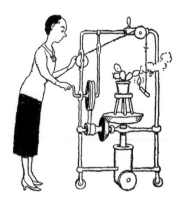

A Handy Device for De-Spiking Cacti

Perfect Form

for use in the de-spiking season. As cacti are difficult plants to prune manually without an occasional oath, this should prove a boon to cactus-lovers who wish to keep their hands fit for golf, lifting tankards or applauding Glamour Girls.)

As most people are aware, plants are either deciduous or not. In other words, either they fall apart in the Autumn and look pretty awful until the following Spring, or they bloom grimly away all the year round. Though the all-round bloomers are seldom as decorative as the wilters, it is a good plan to have a few of them in every garden, to lessen the latter's resemblance to a municipal rubbish-dump during the months November—March. Laurels, holly and ivy (which can be grown by anybody with a house to grow it on), are probably the best for this purpose.

Re flowers, now. Before planting so much as a solitary buttercup—which would look dashed silly, anyway—the gardener should give some thought to the general colour-scheme that will result when everything (to his astonishment) has come up. A garden containing only red flowers, for example, is an affront to the eye and a menace to the peace of the home, the irritant effect of red upon the nerve-centres being well known to psychologists, bulls and the retired military. In the same way, an all-white garden tends to induce snow-blindness in the family and neighbours, while an all-yellow one just looks bilious.

The gardener, then, must either work out a preliminary colour-scheme himself or hire a local artist for a small sum in bronze. As a foundation, a few roses, tulips and/or dahlias are generally useful, as these can be had in several pleasing shades and always look well in vases. Among roses, my personal favourites are Mrs. Wapshott (light crimson: very sweet), Lady Bilch-Overspoon (glossy rose: most abundant and continuous bloomer), Prunella Simpson (pink: large), Fifi Mechante (creamy pink: very free and beautiful),

Reviving a Wilted Plant

General Quacklingham (rich velvety crimson: very strong), and O. J. W. Featheringstonehamptonhaugh (salmon pink: large white eye). Apart from the two last, a jollier bunch of girls one could not hope to meet.

His roses selected, and his tulips and dahlias added to taste, the gardener can turn his attention to his hardy annuals—those tough little growths which can be trusted to do their stuff with the minimum of supervision. The most popular of these, at the moment, are phlox, sox, clarkia elegans (named, I believe, after that Mr. Clark who introduced spats into England), larkspur, love-in-a-mist, fun-in-a-belfry, coreopsis, ellipsis, mignonette, candytuft, bishop's-nightshirt, nasturtium and echsol . . . eschscol . . . (Just a moment, please) . . . eschscholtzia. The last-named, which is pronounced

Removing Worn-Out Teeth from a Rake

Root-Pruning

like a walrus sneezing through a double thickness of felt after a heavy meal on a murky evening in Kirkcudbright, is generally spelt "Cal-i-for-ni-an pop-py", to the relief of all.

These sturdy little fellows can be left out in the open in all weathers and need little attention, even at the height of an English summer, apart from an occasional kind word or tot of water. There are other flowers, however, whose frail constitutions require careful nursing, particularly in the winter, in what are commonly known as "greenhouses"—possibly because they have little in common with the average house and are not invariably green.

The drawback to greenhouses, from the point of view of those who perspire freely, is that they are dashed hot inside, the idea being (a) to keep the floral inmates warm when blizzards rage without, and (b) to encourage by the Turkish Bath process any plants that

A Handy Attachment for the Greenhouse

seem reluctant to grow up. As a result, stout gardeners are apt to gasp considerably in greenhouses, and even to dwindle physically, thus getting themselves tittered at by anybody within eyeshot.

To meet this difficulty, Mr. Heath Robinson has kindly designed an attachment (see illustration) which can be fitted to any greenhouse in less time than it takes to say so. This is simply a kind of tent in which, unobserved by the neighbours, gardeners who feel the heat can exchange their winter woollies for the latest in water-wear before plunging into the inferno to give their orchids the once-over.

Those who, having gambled away their inheritance or invested their all in a Siberian sponge-mine, cannot afford a full-sized greenhouse, will find the miniature model, here depicted, well worth their attention. This will accommodate simultaneously one adult and a couple of tomatoes, and can be carried under the arm when circumstances—such as a failure to pay the rent or a rumour that the police have got wind of the coining-plant in the basement—necessitate a quick removal to Tahiti.

So much for the vital First Step—the actual choice of flowers. If the young gardener has carefully followed the instructions here set forth, he should now have, on the one hand, an utterly defenceless garden, and, on the other, a bewildering assortment of bulbs, seeds and cuttings. While he is inserting the latter in the former, prodding a hole there and a hole there and humming a gay snatch of song, we will turn—after a short interval for cocoa, etc.—to the subject of Gardens, The Care And Maintenance Of.

We thank you, one and all.

Pocket Greenhouse

Weeding without Treading on the Beds

Thawing the Ground

CARE OF THE GARDEN

The young gardener—or "Eric", as we will call him, for a change—must not suppose that his labours are completed when he has planted all his flora and/or veg., and that he can just sit back and wait for things to sprout. For Nature, in her inscrutable wisdom, has decreed that where there is a garden there shall also be (a) a lot of weeds and (b) a good deal of insect-life, red in tooth and claw and capable of eating anything from a pansy to a hollyhock; and these must be persuaded of the error of their ways, if necessary by force.

Weeds, if left to riot unchecked, can overrun a garden in less time than it takes to say: "*Xerophyllum Asphodeloides*, the famous Athenian philosopher", and must therefore be ruthlessly nipped in the bud. Merely to wrench the top off a weed, leaving its roots to fester

How to De-Thistle and Re-Sow a Lawn in One Movement

underground, is to ensure that the beastly thing will bloom again at its earliest convenience; the whole growth, ganglions and all, must be scooped aside and either flung over the fence or used to stuff cushions, etc.

Owing to the amount of stooping involved, weeding is no task for the aged or infirm; and even those who are still fairly flexible about the middle will find the Heath Robinson "Peter Pan" Eeziweeda a very present help. This, as the illustration shows, is a kind of small travelling-crane of one-woman-power, which enables the weedsman to take the weight off his feet and quarter the garden thoroughly without treading on the flower-beds and injuring the tulip-crop. Probably the most superfluous of all weeds is the thistle, a Scottish parasite which can be as great a nuisance in Putney as in Peebles. It is possible, however, to de-thistle and re-sow a lawn almost in one movement with the help of a small donkey and a barrel of grass-seed (see diagram). The fact that donkeys actually like eating thistles suggests that their reputation for nitwittery is not wholly undeserved.

As insects, unlike weeds, are loth to stand still and let the gardener rebuke them, it is often necessary to employ guile when coping with the earwigs, wireworms, greenfly, weevils, blight, cabbage-butterflies, ants, woodlice, cockchafers, daddys-long-legs (? daddy-long-legses) and other aphides which, if allowed to multiply and have fun, can make the toughest garden look extremely second-hand.

Earwigs, for example, are notoriously shy on the wing, but as they have little intelligence they can usually be dealt with in the manner here shown. Lured to the trap by a trail of caviare or some similar delicacy, the little creatures can easily be stunned with a mallet and either deported to the next garden or throttled with a bootlace, as the mood of the

The Earwig Trap

Killing Greenfly

moment suggests. In the same way, by disguising himself as a rose-tree—a simple task for anybody with a little spare time and a slight sense of histrionics—the gardener can often inveigle a greenfly within striking-distance and deal it a fatal buffet with the ingenious apparatus here depicted. (Those who object to these expedients on humanitarian grounds are asked to remember that these little pests fulfil no useful purpose in the scheme of things. They exist, indeed, merely to annoy, as anybody will testify who has ever flushed a clutch of earwigs from the turn-up of his trousers.)

Most of the insects that infest gardens are oddly susceptible to the scent of tobacco, and will fall into a swoon on being briskly smoked at or sprayed with powdered snuff; once unconscious, they can be packed in bundles of ten and forwarded to the Chancellor of the Exchequer in the guise of "conscience-money". When employing the snuff-gambit, the gardener—to avoid spraying the people next door, and thereby giving rise to ill-feeling and possibly the exchange of invective—is advised to use the curvilinear re-entrant type of snuff-spray, as illustrated, thus ensuring that any resultant sneezing-fits will occur on his side of the fence.

Those insects, such as the wireworm (so called because it resembles a short piece of wire: a striking instance of *le mot juste*), which attack the roots of plants require rather more elaborate treatment. As even a wireworm must occasionally come to the surface for air, it can sometimes be trapped by burying a small portion of turnip in such a position that the insect is practically bound to notice it on the way up and pause for a light snack; it is then a simple matter to exhume both wireworm and turnip, consign the former to the flames and return the latter to the larder.

Wireworms with no taste for turnips are best abolished by the subterranean gas-attack method devised by Mr. Heath Robinson and depicted here. The necessary apparatus consists of an old meerschaum, an ounce of shag, a kettle and a length of rubber tubing, the kettle being secretly buried near the roots of the threatened plant and shag-fumes discharged through

The Re-Entrant Snuff-Spray

it at the luckless insect by an experienced shag-smoker. After five minutes of this treatment, the stoutest wireworm that ever ate a privet-hedge is apt to wish that it had been born a seagull.

Mention of seagulls reminds me that thoughtless birds can do considerable damage to a garden. Our feathered friends—and notably the sparrow, the starling, the common vulture, the cloth-eared nutjar, and the greater whey-faced piefinch, or Peabody's Puffin—have no respect for innocent young flowers and regard a newly sown lawn as a kind of quick-lunch counter. A fine-meshed net, covering the entire garden, will usually baffle these marauders; but many gardeners, contending that this lets in the rain and interferes with the tennis, prefer to discourage them with buckshot.

*Asphyxiating a Wireworm at the Root
of a Favourite Plant*

CARE OF THE GARDEN

Birds Can Do Considerable Damage

A more humane method, perhaps, is to engage a qualified bird-scarer, or dance-band vocalist, trained to scare birds by twirling a police-rattle and crying "Shoo! Shoo!" at regular intervals. If this is impracticable for economic reasons, one can get the same result by installing half a dozen loud-speakers at strategic points about the garden and connecting them to a microphone in the dining-room. By this means the gardener can roar abuse at intrusive pelicans and other wildfowl without interrupting his meals.

As havoc-wreckers in gardens, dogs and cats can be pretty effective, too, unless carefully watched. Dogs will be dogs, of course, but their habit of interring bones in flower-beds in order to dig them up again does no good to the local bulbage. As for cats, these have a remarkable propensity for infesting other people's estates, and can make even a wet February night more hideous than it ordinarily is by their weakness for vocalism. As old boots and other missiles thrown at cats seldom hit the target, particularly at night, Mr. Heath Robinson has designed a simple self-operating machine, known as the Ever-Ready Cat-dowser, for the benefit of the cat-ridden. As the diagram shows, the victim, attracted by the bait, leaps unsuspectingly upon a small platform, which immediately decants the animal into a well-filled hip-bath and simultaneously anoints it with a bucketful of used bath-water, to its surprise and indignation. One encounter with this ingenious gadget will convert the boldest cat that ever stole a turbot into a nervous wreck; and it would probably have the same effect on duns and rate-collectors, if any such could be persuaded to try it.

The Micro Bird-Scarer

CARE OF THE GARDEN

Gardeners who are greatly plagued by slugs are advised to lay in a tortoise. These lovable and not uncomely little creatures—which, when fully extended, so closely resemble almost any well-known statesman with a secret sorrow—can be bought for as little as sixpence each and provide endless fun for the

The Cat-Dowser

kiddies. The cost of maintaining a tortoise is almost negligible, as the moment it is turned loose in the garden it will disappear for about six months; but the moral effect of its presence on the local slugs is wholly salutary. Gardeners who have not hitherto had much social intercourse with tortoises are warned against confusing them with turtles, as the latter are not only more expensive and much larger, but considerably more eclectic in their tastes—for which, as they are merely soup-in-embryo, one can hardly blame them.

A Midnight Snail-Hunt With a Trained Tortoise

HOW TO MAKE A GARDEN GROW

The above observations, naturally, apply only to British gardens, where wild beasts and venomous reptiles are seldom seen by the abstemious, and where the gardener is rarely required to face anything more deadly than an embittered slug, a clutch of casual cats, or a caterpillar maddened by over-indulgence in lettuce. In India, Africa and other over-heated spots the horticulturist's task is greatly complicated by the vipers, wild boars, stray hippopotami and similar fauna which keep turning up among his wallflowers. Thus, although the resident in the tropics can grow things unheard-of by his British confrere—lotus, for example, and real coconuts, and the rare bifocal banyan, or Pinwhistle's pansy—the knowledge that at any moment his trowel may dislodge a sleeping leopard or bring a python about his ears does no good to his nervous system.

As this book is intended primarily for home consumption—though it can also be used to prop up the legs of pianos—I do not feel called upon to deal with such problems here, the more so as the abatement of leopards, etc., is hardly gardening, in the true sense of that word.

Testing Sap-Pressure

48

Borrowing

THE SEASONS

It is wrong to suppose, as many do, that a garden needs attention only in the summer, and that for the remainder of the year the young horticulturist can devote his leisure exclusively to card-games, amateur bacteriology or the rearing of pedigree newts. If it is to give of its best, a garden must be cherished all the year round as carefully as if it were an aged and affluent aunt with no other relatives. In other words, the gardener must be almost continuously on the job, toiling, rejoicing and borrowing occasional implements from a kindly neighbour.

Of the four (4) seasons, that which is heralded by the cuckoo is probably the most fascinating to the true

Sowing and Watering a New Lawn

garden-addict. The cuckoo, notwithstanding its anti-social habit of laying other birds' eggs in its own nest, is Spring's appointed harbinger; and its peculiar glue-like shriek is the signal for Mother Earth to wake from her long winter sleep and develop a rash of primroses and what not. A few pushful young flowers, it is true, make their appearance before Spring has been well and truly harbinged; but the cuckoo is generally regarded as the official starter.

The flowers that bloom in the Spring (what ho!) must obviously have been planted some time previously, but those which refuse to be bustled, preferring to blossom later in the year, usually start life as seeds or bulbs in April, or thereabouts. Now is the time, therefore, for all good men to come to the aid of the garden by planting the chrysanthemums, cornflowers, delphiniums, sweet peas, love-lies-bleedings, who-goes-theres, forget-me-nots and kiss-me-quicks which—if they have the luck to escape exhumation in their infancy by the local dog-life—will evoke gasps of admiration from visitors in July and August.

While so engaged, the gardener will be cheered and encouraged by the appearance of those flowers—primroses, cowslips, daffodils and the like—which have contrived to sprout without any assistance from him. In every keen gardening household the arrival of the first daffodil is a definite event, almost comparable in excitement value to the discovery of a new oil-well. Since the average daffodil, however, is quite noiseless, its blooming is liable to pass unremarked by the unobservant or preoccupied. To obviate this risk, Mr. Heath Robinson has designed an apparatus whereby the eagerly awaited blossom can announce its arrival to all. This is simply a second-hand concertina, fitted with a suitable tune and a small loud-speaker, and ingeniously operated by the daffodil itself, as shown. Summoned by this tocsin, the family has ample time

The Daff-Indicator for Giving Notice of First Appearance

to rush out and assume admiring postures round the precious newcomer.

As subjects for poesy, Spring flowers have always been extremely popular. Who, for example, does not know the exquisite "Dawn Over Magnesia", by Aloysius Fyshe, which begins:

> "Hark! The plumbago is in bud!
> And, gosh! The genteel crocus
> Burgeons like any wombat's blood!
> Can Life be out of focus
> When rhododendra bloom anew
> And there are Gardens still at Kew?"

As the majority of poets live in one-room flats or rat-infested garrets, their opportunities for seeking floral inspiration are rather limited. The garden-owner, therefore, who wishes to combine altruism with business can simultaneously benefit mankind and collect a few odd ducats by admitting poets, in small selected batches, to his garden on fine Spring afternoons and letting them brood there until their respective Muses have kicked in with the needful. For this facility the most impoverished verse-maker will gladly pay at the rate of, say, one shilling per brood-hour.

During the Summer, when there is little actual planting to be done, the gardener's

Subject for Poesy

Garden Kindness

chief duty is to protect his pleasaunce from the vagaries of the weather. The British climate being what it is, it is no rare thing for a typical July day to be immediately followed by an unmistakable December ditto. Thus plants of frail physique—i.e., not the aspidistra—are likely to perish in their prime of either thirst or drowning unless they are carefully watched.

On warm, sunny days it is only necessary to throw water, to which a dash of orange bitters may be added, upon them from time to time. Gardeners who object on political or moral grounds to paying a heavy water-rate will find second-hand bath-water quite suitable for this purpose, a slight *soupçon* of soap being appreciated by phlox and fuchsia alike. In very hot weather the gardener who adopts this expedient will have to take rather more baths than he perhaps considers necessary, but he will have the consolation of knowing

Forcing the Aspidistra

53

Safety Attachment for Storms

that he is simultaneously refreshing his violets, giving the local Water Board a nasty smack in the eye, and imparting to himself that pinkly glowing appearance which is the hallmark of the Well-Scrubbed Man.

As bath-water that has been carried about by hand in saucepans and fire-buckets lacks the energizing qualities of that which is pumped direct from bath to consumer, Mr. Heath Robinson has designed an apparatus (see diagram) whereby the healing fluid, having finished job A in the bathroom, can be transferred without delay to the garden and encouraged to get on with job B. This gadget is so simple that a child can make it—any child, that is, who has the necessary pipery, bellowage and mechanical turn of mind.

Protection from the Tempest

A Pump for Using the Bath Water in the Garden

During the cold spells and periods of stormy weather so characteristic of the English summer, different and more drastic measures must be taken. These include the provision of inexpensive umbrellas to shield innocent young shrubs from sudden tempests, the attachment of lightning-conductors to the hats of such garden-lovers as cannot be persuaded to come in out of the wet, and the swaddling of valuable rose-trees against chill zephyrs from the east.

For swaddling purposes, old trousers, discarded hats, outmoded nightshirts and similar surplus garments will be found very handy. A trousered rose-tree may be considered giggleworthy by the thoughtless; but its owner, knowing that the iciest blasts are beating in vain against his Viscountess Twombley (rosy pink, excellent when pegged down) and his P. Bootlady, Esq. (dark crimson, perpetual hybrid), need lose no sleep on that account.

Swaddling Tender Plants

The Boreas-Baffler

Where old trousers are lacking—in exclusively Scottish households, for example—small revolving windscreens, or Boreas-bafflers, worked by chastely-designed weathercocks, can be fitted to such plants as seem to need them; and very elegant they look, believe us.

Attention should also be paid at this season to creepers of all sorts, as these tend to get out of hand and creep not wisely, but too well. Nothing so becomes a house as a top-dressing of virginia creeper, but unless the latter is periodically checked it is apt to sneak in at the windows and turn up in the oddest places, such as the bathroom, to the confusion of those who happen to be there at the time.

With the coming of Autumn, a certain melancholy attacks the ardent horticulturist, causing him to sigh a good deal and refuse his porridge; for it is then that his treasured garden begins to fall apart. One by one the flowers that made so brave a show in August begin to wither and turn black round the edges, while the risk of being stunned by falling leaves adds a new hazard to the daily tour of the estate.

The saddening influence of falling leaves has often been remarked on by poets who have run out of Spring material. By many leading thinkers it is attributed to the fact that they (the leaves, not the thinkers, unfortunately) have to be swept up and thrown away—gruelling work for the obese and conducive to pains in the back. As the accompanying illustration shows, however, leaf-lovers and unwilling benders can

Keeping the Leaves On

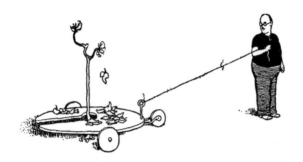

Catching Fallen Leaves Without Littering the Garden

postpone this task almost indefinitely by securing every leaf within reach to its parent twig by means of stout twine or a powerful fixative. This gives the foliage a longer lease of life and leads myopic neighbours to conclude that their clocks are at least a month fast.

Those who regard this practice as—well, let's face it—cheating, but who nevertheless consider leaf-collecting one of Life's grimmer jobs, should be interested in Mr. Heath Robinson's ingenious Anti-Stoop Leafcatcher, here shown. With the help of this device falling leaves can be intercepted *before they reach the ground* and conveyed almost in the same movement to the site appointed for the bonfire which, to be perfectly candid, is half the fun of gardening. A somewhat similar principle underlies the suggested method, also depicted, of protecting windfalls from those abrasions which spoil their appearance and impair their value as pie-matter.

If Autumn is a depressing season for the garden-lover, Winter is even more so, and then some. In

Preventing the Windfall from Bruising

November, December, and January the average garden looks about as gay as a wet Sunday in Glasgow; nor is there anything that the gardener can do about it, apart from rolling the lawn, weeding the paths and inviting a few friends occasionally for a day's slug-shooting.

All the same, Mr. Heath Robinson and I feel that gardeners despair too easily in Winter. After all, the British are a pretty hardy race—witness their unshakable affection for boiled cabbage—with a passion for fresh air that is worth thousands annually to Harley Street; and with a little care and ingenuity a garden can be made almost as attractive in December as in June. All that is required is (or are) a few artificial flowers—preferably made of tin, to withstand hailstorms—one or two imitation rose-trees in frost-proof zinc, a little synthetic heat in the form of portable

60

A Winter Garden

oil-stoves, plenty of umbrellas, a lot of imagination, some stout boots and a set of warm woollen underwear for everybody.

Given these props., one can have fun in the garden even in mid-Winter. Croquet can be played between showers, invigorating walks taken, dummy admiration bestowed upon the dummy roses, and life in general enjoyed as if Nature were still in bloom.

As neither Mr. Heath Robinson nor I have as yet put this theory to the test, owing partly to our fear of chilblains and partly to our gardenless condition, we trust that somebody will give it a trial on our behalf, and advise us of the upshot, outcome or result.

A Dibbing
Chair

The Onion-Bed

THE KITCHEN-GARDEN

The difference between a parsnip grown at home and one acquired from a greengrocer is not simply one of price; there is the sentimental angle to be considered. A vegetable that one has personally tended, with loving hands and unremitting care, from innocent seedhood to rich maturity, must obviously have a stronger claim on the affections than one which is merely delivered at the back door by an oafish youth on a bicycle.

For this reason many British gardeners are apt to feel occasionally that they would like to grow some vegetables, if only for the rather melancholy pleasure of eating something that they have known all its life. Well, thanks to Mr. Heath Robinson and myself (Mr. R., incidentally, is the one in the smarter hat), this ambition need no longer remain unfulfilled. A careful study of the following pages should enable anybody of average intelligence, and even those who excelled at games at school, to grow sufficient green-stuff for his personal needs. By so doing, maybe, he will earn the enmity of his greengrocer, but he will save quite a lot of money which can be devoted to some worthy cause, such as the provision of reversible ear-muffs for salesmen of water-softeners on the North Polar circuit.

According to the experts—those enviable souls who were born with silver trowels in their mouths and a mulching-iron in each chubby fist—a kitchen-garden should always be considerably longer than it is wide. Unwilling though we are to appear baffled, we simply cannot explain this whimsy—unless the idea is that in oblong gardens there is more elbow-room for marrows than in square ones. Anyway, there it is; and the greater length should always be from east to west—never from north to south. This (as a little calculation with slide-rule and protractor will convince the dumbest) is to ensure that the vegetables concerned get their full share of healing sunlight, which is as essential to an artichoke as to an architect —rather more so, in fact, as many architects blister easily.

For the benefit of keen vegetarians who have not much land at their disposal, there is appended a gull's-eye view of a compact kitchen-garden designed by Mr. Heath Robinson (in collaboration with the Brothers Karamazov, here shown) to yield the maximum of assorted veg. from the minimum of ground. It will be observed that in this attractive little layout room has been found not only for a potting-shed—adaptable for use as an air-raid shelter or a place to let home-made

Economical Layout of a Kitchen Garden

Mushroom Spawn—That Was!

cheese mature in—but also for the bonfire without which no gardener's autumn is complete. Those who do not care for curly kale—I don't, for one—can plant hibiscus, which, though inedible, will impart a pleasingly *outré* appearance to the scene and can be worn behind the ear by the female members of the family.

Naturally, in deciding what vegetables to grow, the kitchen-gardener must be guided by his personal tastes and those of his nearest and dearest. If, for example, he is at all like Mr. Heath Robinson and myself, he will plant no spinach; on the other hand, he will plant a good deal of asparagus. That is, if he is lucky, asparagus being a pretty tricky plant and not easily cultivated by beginners. The latter, indeed, are advised first to try their strength and get their eye in on something simpler, such as potatoes, which are said to have been introduced into England by Sir Walter Raleigh and can be served boiled, mashed, fried or *saute*, as desired.

It is a mistake, by the way, to devote the entire kitchen-garden to one species of vegetable, and one only. However crazy one may be about cucumber, for example, it is unwise to grow nothing else, as the appearance of this eel-like delicacy at every meal, with never a spring onion or a Nutting's Dwarf Red Beetroot to break the monotony, is bound in time to provoke unrest in the most docile household. "A little of everything, with any luck" should be the gardener's motto, with the corollary: "And everything in its place", since any attempt to grow parsley on a currant-bush is foredoomed to failure.

Mention of spring onions reminds me that it is often difficult for the not-so-agile gardener to thin out these little creatures without trampling all over the bed, thus getting his boots full of earth and doing more harm than good. This difficulty can be overcome by the use of a pair of stilts and the simple apparatus here depicted. Not everybody, admittedly, is a natural stilt-walker, but with a few hours' practice in a public park or deserted seaplane hangar almost anybody should be able to remain aloft long enough for this purpose.

Among the more spectacular vegetables is the marrow, a member of the well-known, influential and justly popular Gourd family. With the right kind of upbringing, a marrow will attain astonishing dimensions, and can be used for boasting purposes in clubs, saloon-bars, and the salons of Mayfair. The shapelier the

Thinning out the Spring Onions

67

Ensuring Good Shape in Marrows

marrow, the better its chances of winning handsome silver cups at flower-shows; and a pair of pre-War corsets—such as may be found, even nowadays, in almost every lumber-room and on a few conservative old aunts—will prove helpful in training its contours in the way that they should go. Apart from its rather eerie habit of creeping about the garden and sending out long shoots to snare the unwary foot, the marrow is a well-behaved and easy-growing plant; while it has the further advantage that—in the evening of its days, when it has retired, full of honours, from the show-ring—it can be dropped from upper windows upon the heads of duns.

A word *re* strawberries, while I think of it. Although these are not vegetables in the true sense of the word, it is a poor kitchen-gardener who has never tried to grow some. The difficulty here, of course, is to ensure that the person detailed to pick the little rascals does not devour more than he collects, as the mere act of picking a strawberry engenders a craving to eat it. As Freud points out, however, in his *How To Go Crazy* (in six fortnightly parts), this psychological problem can usually be solved by a piece of stout strawberry-proof canvas, lashed firmly about the picker's lower face in such a manner as to thwart his subconscious urge.

The question of fertilization—by which I mean (I think) the pepping-up of plants by the transfer of pollen from one to another—is frequently a stumbling-block to the novice gardener. How the deuce (he is apt to ask himself, frowning nervously and tugging his moustache) does one transfer pollen, exactly? Grain by grain, with the forefinger and thumb? In bundles of ten, by sheer personal magnetism? Or how?

*Safety Attachment for Use When
Picking Strawberries*

The Pollen Blower

Well, two fairly simple methods are illustrated here. In the case of very tall vegetables (that shown in the diagram is the Polynesian glueberry, a very rare plant) a telescopic pollen-blower—which can be constructed in a few moments from an ordinary telescope, part of an egg-whisk and the exit end of a coaching horn—will give the best results. Gardeners of a more whimsical disposition can train a bee, a butterfly, or some such insect that can be trusted to know pollen when it sees it, to do the job for them.

An essential feature of every kitchen-garden is a scarecrow, adolescent vegetables having an irresistible attraction for birds of weak moral fibre. The more life-like the scarecrow, obviously, the greater its efficiency as a frightener of freebooting fowls; but any old Gent's Spring Suiting, stuffed with rook's feathers and surmounted by a disused bowler, will suffice for all ordinary occasions, such refinements as socks and a wrist-watch not being really necessary. Gardeners who have no old clothes, other than those they are wearing, will find that octogenarian uncles in reduced circumstances are usually willing, for a small consideration, to take over the scarecrow's duties.

Carrying Pollen from one Plant to Another by Means of a Trained Butterfly

71

The "Kigarbox" or Kitchen Garden Window-Box

THE KITCHEN-GARDEN

A Lifelike Scarecrow

The urge to grow one's own vegetables is not, of course, peculiar to householders; flat-dwellers often experience it, too. Although kitchen-gardening on a large scale is impossible to the latter, they can go in for it in a quiet way with the help of the Heath Robinson "Kigarbox" (or kitchen-garden-window-box). The *deluxe* model, here illustrated, is divided into moth-proof compartments, each designed to accommodate one (1) vegetable. Thus, the flat-dweller who has a catholic taste in veg. can grow a carrot, a radish, a turnip, an onion, a potato, a pea and a broad bean more or less simultaneously and with hardly any effort, happily aware that—with the help of a little mutton— he can produce a nourishing stew for one person at any hour of the day or night.

In the limited space at our disposal it is impossible for Mr. Heath Robinson and/or myself to cover every aspect of the kitchen-garden racket, even if we had the necessary knowledge and inclination. But if the foregoing hints prove to be of no value whatever to Britain's ambitious young potato-fans and artichoke-addicts, we shall feel—to put it bluntly—that it is no fault of ours.

Magnetic Braces

Design for a Landscape Garden

ROCK-GARDENS, ROOF-GARDENS, ETC.

The desire to build a rockery lies dormant in every true gardener's heart, protected from the elements by his stout woollen vest and needing only a little encouragement to bring it to the surface. That encouragement is here and now supplied by Mr. Heath Robinson and myself, if not exactly free of charge, at least at a price within the reach of the most modest purse.

There is no doubt that a well-planned rock-garden, rich in *arabis*, *aubretia*, *alyssum*, *arenaria*, old Uncle *Armeria* and all, adds a touch of distinction to the premises and solves the problem of What To Do With That Corner By The Dustbin. Rock-plants, moreover, are mostly of Alpine origin and consequently pretty tough; having once been persuaded to start sprouting, they need little further coddling, apart from an occasional kind word and tot of water. Nor is this surprising, for

Snowdon

by comparison with the rigours of life on the top of an Alp, the amenities of a back-garden existence must seem positively Paradisal.

Without a sufficiency of rocks, of course, no rockery can be anything but a mockery. The gardener can either buy this essential stonework from a reliable rock-dealer, or (if his means are limited) collect it during his summer holidays over a period of years—now purloining a small portion of Stonehenge, now furtively snaffling the extreme apex of Mount Snowdon, and now filching the odd paving-stone when the Borough Surveyor is not looking. That done, he has only to arrange his material in a decorative heap, fill in the cracks with earth, plant his *erinus alpinus*, his *ramondia pyrenaica* and his *arpeggio absurdum* (or Alpine nut-rose), and let Nature do the rest. Gardeners' feet on which chunks of rock have been dropped during the proceedings can usually be soothed by liniment; and any such chunks that are left over can be used as door-stops, paper-weights, emergency tie-presses, or things to throw at cats in the night-watches.

It is said that in the year 1887 a M. Aristide Hippolyte Jean-Marie Bop, then head-waiter at "Seaview", Railway Avenue, Shivering-on-

A Small Portion of Stonehenge

Sea, inadvertently let fall a large soufflé-dish upon the parquet; whereupon he exclaimed "Eureka!" and broke into a jig, having invented crazy-paving. Be that as it may, or not, the fact remains that (like any rural dean and his fiancée) rock-gardens and crazy-paving often go hand-in-hand, the one providing a fitting background for the other, and the other affording a means of access to the one.

To be perfectly frank, a crazy-pavement is merely an ordinary pavement that has been brutally assaulted with a hammer; but a little of it lends tone to any garden, while the mental exercise involved in fitting it together keeps the gardener's mind alert and gives him a taste for jigsaw-puzzlery that will stand him in good stead whenever he is convalescing from pneumonia, ingrowing dyspepsia, or a goat-butt at the base of the spine.

*Inventor of Crazy Paving
First Getting the Idea*

From the rock-garden it is but a step—for the abnormally active, at any rate—to the garden on the roof, or "roof-garden", as it is laughingly called, to save time. Not everybody, alas, has ground-floor garden-space at his disposal; but nearly everybody has a roof on which, with a little care and forethought, things can be made to grow.

The flatter the roof, of course, the easier the growing, as Confucius points out in Vol. II of his *Memoirs*. On the roofs of many ultra-modern houses—the sort that look like very large square pieces of rather *passé* cheese—there is room not only for a bed of leeks, a herbaceous border and a miniature grouse-moor, but for a badminton-court, a fishpond and at least two of the tenant's more corpulent uncles. (Should the roof give way beneath this burden, the builders concerned will probably settle out of court rather than expose their joists in public.)

Even on the ordinary or Λ-shaped roof, however, one can lay out a modest pleasaunce that will give delight to all who have a good head for heights and a comprehensive insurance-policy. As the illustration shows, by attaching potted shrubs to prominent chimney-stacks and erecting on the crown of the roof a flat superstructure of rainproof teak, it is possible to cultivate anything from a pansy to a pepper-tree (which is rarely more than five feet high and will contribute generously to the cruet).

The chief advantage of roof-gardens, as opposed to those on *terra firma*, is that they cannot be got at by dogs with a bone-burial complex, or overrun by adolescents in search of strayed tennis-balls. At roof-level, too, the air is considerably fresher and untainted by the scent of boiling cabbage, while extensive views in all directions can be enjoyed by those who like that kind of thing. And finally, the roof-gardener, since he cannot be overlooked by his neighbours, is

An Attractively Laid-Out Roof-Garden

unembarrassed by the latter's ill-concealed contempt for his efforts and their patronizing hints as to the best method of rearing daisies.

As to roof-top rock-gardens, I myself am rather doubtful about these, cautious old sceptic that I am. Mr. Heath Robinson—the obstinate young so-and-so!—insists that a rockery not only improves the appearance of any roof, but acts as a useful bulwark against meteorites, hostile bombs, portly parachutists and similar aerial hazards of this day and age. That may well be; but what if a portion of the rockery, dislodged by a sudden cyclone or a careless foot, comes suddenly unstuck, to impinge with an echoing clang upon the skull of some harmless muffin-vendor or other passer-by? Will not the consequences be such as to make the roof-top gardener wish he had chosen some other hobby, such as collecting matchbox labels?

Candidly, I think so; but those who care to run this risk are referred to the accompanying illustration, which can be cut out, mounted on stiff parchment and used as a novelty lampshade, if desired.

For much the same reason I am not wholly in favour of rock-gardens in window-boxes, as these are also liable to come loose and plunge earthward, causing widespread loss of life. For ordinary purposes, however, the keen horticulturist who has neither roof nor garden on his premises—probably, I'll bet a ducat, because he lives about half-way up one of these modern blocks of flats, with inconstant hot water and everything—will find a window-box a very present help. Almost anything that grows in a garden will grow in a window-box, though naturally in rather smaller numbers. Certain plants—laurels, pumpkins, and the like—are obviously

The Roof Rock-Garden

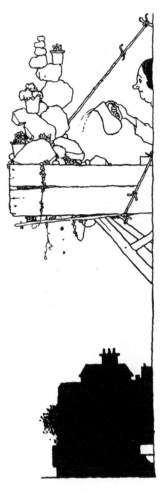

The Window-Box Rockery

unsuitable for window-box cultivation; while certain elongated others — notably sun-flowers and hollyhocks — are also to be avoided, as they not only obscure the view from the window but have a tendency, when fully grown, to catch in the eaves above and push the roof off.

Within these limits, however, window-box-gardening can be fully as enjoyable as the full-sized variety, much easier on the dorsal muscles, and considerably cheaper; for whereas plants for a life-sized garden must be ordered by the dozen, score or gross — much as one orders tintacks or bottles of oatmeal stout — those for a window-box can be bought modestly one by one, as if they were collar-studs or umbrellas.

Well, that, I think, states the case for rock-gardens, roof-gardens, and window-boxes about as fairly as such a case can be stated on a wet afternoon like this. It only remains to add that readers requiring further advice on this or any other subject are advised not to apply to Mr. Heath Robinson or myself (as we are leaving shortly for a holiday on our tandem-cycle), but to the Ministry of Agriculture and Fisheries, enclosing a postal-order for 1s. 3d. as a guarantee of good faith.

Dangerous Tendency

Leaning Post

THE GARDEN BEAUTIFUL

The subject of garden-ornaments—statuary, bird-baths, sundials, etc., is one of interest to all who are interested in that subject. In very small gardens, or gardenettes, a lot of statuary is as obviously out of place as a lot of grandfather-clocks in a bathroom; but, broadly speaking, one may say that a reasonable amount of ornamental stonework adds dignity to the place and enables passing cormorants to sit down and rest their feet.

In selecting statuary for this purpose, the gardener—and his Aunt Honoria, if she is helping him—must be guided by his artistic sense, if any. A life-sized reproduction, in Correra marble, of the Ways and Means Committee of the L.C.C. would look all wrong among the wallflowers and tulips, as would a bronze effigy of a hippopotamus at play. A statue of Eros, on the other hand, goes well with rhododendrons and can be draped with trousers in the wink of an eye when the Vicar calls unexpectedly; while it has the additional advantage that it can be fitted with a cigarette-box for the comfort of those visitors who never smoke their own if they can help it. The same applies, of course, to statues of local celebrities, mythological characters, Miss Shirley Temple, and dear ones who have passed away.

Other methods of combining the useful with the ornamental in this manner are here depicted, regardless of expense, for the guidance of gardeners who like to have it both ways. A sundial that merely tells the time— though very few sundials can be trusted to do even that, in my experience, owing to their ignorance of the Daylight Saving Act—is useful only to those whose watches are permanently in pawn, for one reason or another; but a sundial that combines the functions of

Statuary Attachment for Smokers

The Cocktail Fountain

a timepiece and an ale-vat is useful to almost everybody. Gardeners who are opposed to ale, on the ground that it rots the boots, inflames the nose and induces hallucinations, can substitute lemonade or mulberry-juice or even cold camomile tea; but they will not, we hope, enjoy it quite so much.

In the same way, an ornamental cocktail-fountain, designed to emit Martinis in response to pressure of a knob, is an unexpected and gratifying thing to find in an English garden. Owing to the complicated plumbing involved, this gadget is rather more expensive than the simple sunbeerdial, or sundiale, but it is greatly appreciated by visitors from Mayfair who like an occasional quick one under the blue vault of Heaven.

In recent years the fair face of England has broken out in a horrid rash of little model gnomes, dwarfs, elves and similar whimsicalities in terra-cotta. This is deeply deplored by both

The Sundial Ale-Vat

86

The Gnome Ash-Tray

Mr. Heath Robinson and myself; but, realizing that fifty million gardeners cannot possibly be wrong, we have schooled ourselves to grin and bear it. We do feel, however, that if there *must* be dummy gnomes in gardens, they should do something more than just lie about and trip up the short-sighted.

Some, for example, can be converted into ash-trays, as nothing looks worse in a garden than cigarette-ash carelessly scattered on the lawns and paths. Others, if sufficiently robust, can be used as seats by visiting

Gnome Seats

relatives who wilt under the strain of being shown round the garden. Others, again, can become receptacles for the sandwiches, spare socks, sealing-wax, short bits of string and other oddments which the gardener is likely to need at any moment.

All the same, Mr. Heath Robinson and I—"Castor" and "Pollux", as we are laughingly called by our creditors—contend that one (1) honest bird-bath is worth ten (10) synthetic dwarfs, inasmuch as the latter fill no long-felt want, whereas the former emphatically do, as many prominent penguins attest.

Gnome Litter Receptacle

In the life of every bird there are moments when it craves either a refreshing draught of water or an invigorating wash, or both. Hence the bird-bath, invented on a date that escapes my memory by somebody whose name I cannot recall. Originally, the bird-bath was simply a bowl of water; and a quick glance

Brolly Bird Bath

at the accompanying illustration will show how it has developed, with Mr. Heath Robinson's assistance, during the past few years.

The sample illustrated is the "Heath Robinson Fowl-Operated Kwiksplasche", which can be had on easy terms in a wide range of sizes that will accommodate anything from a condor to a chaffinch. The chief merit of this model is that it is worked entirely by bird-power; all the gardener has to do is to fill the cistern on alternate Fridays. The mechanism, moreover, is so simple that the veriest wren can use it. Merely by sitting in the bath, the travel-stained cuckoo or Tasmanian peewit sets in motion two interlocked self-centred counter-jumping pistons which, aided by a piece of string, operate a small Disch-wasser sponge-valve which, in its turn, revolves once in a clockwise direction to discharge a quart of pure rain-water upon the expectant fowl. (The bird shown in the illustration, incidentally, is a mottled ewe-necked oyster-snatcher, a species remarkable chiefly for its habit of laying square eggs in postmen's hats.) No soap need be provided, nor any loofah; thus the annual cost of maintaining a bird-bath of this kind is considerably less than that of a set of turquoise trouser-buttons.

Topiary, which—unless I am confusing it with toxophily, which is quite possible—is the art or science of distorting bushes into amusing shapes, is a fascinating hobby for an enterprising gardener. There is little about an ordinary bush to compel the eye or evoke the gasp of admiration; but a bush that has been pruned into the semblance of Mr. Winston Churchill or a bloodhound in full cry has a definite entertainment-value and is eagerly nested in by aesthetically minded fowls.

Unlike punting, tracheotomy and playing the Nigerian nose-flute, topiary is almost as easy to do as it is to spell. All the practitioner needs, in fact, is a stout pair of topiary-scissors and

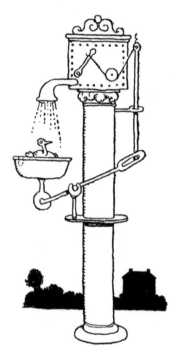

The Fowl-Operated
Kwiksplasche
Bird Bath

Suitable Topiary Designs

a clear mental picture of what he is aiming at; thus equipped, he can carve a box-hedge or a yew-tree into the likeness of anything from his favourite uncle to a fecundity* of rabbits. Retired hairdressers, for obvious reasons, make the best topiarists, but almost anybody with a slight sense of proportion can mould a gorse-bush closer to his heart's desire. It should be remembered, however, that a topiarized bush needs pretty constant attention, as Nature has no respect for Art and is apt—usually at night, when nobody is looking—to add extra twigs, etc., which may ruin the whole effect by giving it a faintly improper look.

It may not be generally known—and even if it is, there is no harm in rubbing it in—that a public

---

* O. Eng. noun of assembly. Cf. "a boast of actors," "a penury of authors," etc.

The Blessing

telephone-booth, modelled on the completely air-proof type provided by the Post Office for people who wish to communicate rapidly with bookmakers—makes an attractive garden ornament. Fashioned of rustic woodwork, painted a restful shade of green and stationed where it cannot fail to catch the eye, it acts as a convenient roosting-site for ivy and enables the gardener to back his fancy, send Christmas Greetings to friends in Venezuela, and ascertain what there is for dinner without going back to the house: a great boon to one who sets a value on his time or suffers with his feet.

I had intended at this juncture to say something scholarly about gazebos, their cause, prevention and cure. There was a time, I understand, when a garden without a gazebo was as rare as a roeless herring; but nowadays they are not so frequently encountered — possibly because only the higher ranks of the intelligentsia know what a gazebo is. Even I, until quite recently, was under the impression that gazebos had thick, greyish fur and roamed the African veldt in awe-

*Rustic Wood
Telephone Box*

inspiring herds; and although, thanks to Mr. Heath Robinson's encyclopaedia, I know better now, I have not had time to mug the subject up sufficiently to deal with it here.

In any case, Mr. Heath Robinson and I both feel that, so far as this chapter is concerned, we have done quite enough for the money.

*Garden
Ornament*

The Rock Pool

GARDEN ENTERTAINMENTS

There is clearly not much point in having a well-groomed garden, rich in flora, snails and what not, if one cannot use it to arouse the envy of the less fortunate. The best way of doing this is to inveigle the latter into the garden and then show them round it; but as many people, on learning that they are about to be shown round somebody else's garden, recall urgent appointments elsewhere and make a hurried exit, it is a good plan to provide some form of entertainment that will act, so to speak, as the sugar disguising the pill.

Exactly why it is so wearying to the spirit to be shown round a garden it is difficult to say; but the explanation may be that, to an enthusiastic gardener, his hollyhocks and pansies are the noblest that ever came out of a seed, whereas to the casual observer—whose feet are probably hurting him—they manifestly are not. Keen gardeners, moreover, are apt to prattle at great length on non-existent subjects, such as the petunias which looked so marvellous less than a month ago ("I do *wish* you could have seen them, Mrs. Wapshott!") and the arbutus which is due to create a local sensation in less than a month's time ("I'm *so* sorry you won't be here to see it, Miss Bunfarthing!").

That sort of thing sends non-gardening visitors into a kind of unhappy coma from which they emerge only when they hear somebody operating a siphon; while visitors who have gardens of their own are either attacked by jealousy, in which case they simply sulk, or so swollen with superiority ("You ought to see *my* dahlias, old boy!") that they become offensive and have to be asked to leave.

By staging, however, a garden-party, charity-tea, tennis-binge or similar genteel frolic in it, a garden can be exhibited painlessly but firmly to as many persons as it will accommodate. Garden-parties, roughly speaking, are of two chief types: the large and formal, where top hats are *de rigueur* and real cream is served with the strawberries, and the small and matey, where odd socks are regarded more as an amusing jest than as a social crime; and the gardener concerned must make his arrangements accordingly—remembering that, with the help of a shoe-horn, the co-operation of all present, and a professional trombonist, quite a large and formal party can be fitted into quite a small and matey garden, as the illustration shows.

As most garden-parties occur in the middle of the afternoon, it is fortunately unnecessary to furnish a roast ox or a dozen gross of oysters for the nourishment of the guests. Tea and buns (assorted), however, should always be provided, with lemonade for those

GARDEN ENTERTAINMENTS

A Small Garden Party

who hold that tea converts the lining of the stomach into leather. Sardine-sandwiches are always useful on these occasions, while it is a good plan to set aside a few eclairs for the more notorious bores among the company, inasmuch as nobody can simultaneously eat an eclair and talk about his sciatica.

HOW TO MAKE A GARDEN GROW

How a Dustbin Can be Disguised

Many small-scale gardeners are too dustbin-conscious ever to give garden-parties. The dustbin is one of Life's major necessities, but it does not allure the eye as does the Taj Mahal; nor can it be hurriedly hidden in the day-nursery, as can the family washing, when visitors are sighted on the skyline. Nevertheless, it is quite possible to disguise even a dustbin so that it will remain unidentified by the most lynx-eyed observer. A few pots of foxgloves, aspidistra, rhomboidal cactus or—as in the example shown—*buphthalmum speciosum* (or Clutterbuck's catnip) will transform what is, at heart, an eyesore into something at which the most fastidious visitor will be pleased to look.

An Innocent Deception

Bathing-Pool

A similar innocent artifice may be practised by the gardener whose sunflowers or lupins have been flattened by a thoughtless tempest. Lashed to stout bean-sticks in such a way that the subterfuge is not apparent (see diagram), the moribund flowers—or, if they have been wrecked beyond repair, models of them in coloured aluminium—can be trusted to play their part and deceive the short-sighted guest. As Emerson remarks in his essay on the home-life of the common newt, all's fair in love, war, politics, high finance, ice-hockey and horticulture.

Though organised games are not essential to the success of a garden-party, they help to pass the time and ensure that the guests will not remain glued to the tea-table, eating doggedly, until Night casts her sable mantle o'er the sylvan scene.

Bathing-facilities, if such can be devised, are very helpful here. Quite a small bathing-pool will do, as it is just as refreshing to bathe one at a time as to plunge in in serried cohorts. As a tribute to their cloth, the local clergy should be invited to leap first into the fluid, the

Bob-Apple

The Game of Sock-Marrow

other guests queuing up in accordance with their age, seniority and political influence.

The traditional old games that have made Britain what she is today—or what she was yesterday, if you feel that way about it—accord admirably with the garden-party spirit and afford healthy fun for young and old alike. The most popular, probably, are hide-and-seek, postman's-knock, verger's-holiday (in which each player impersonates a well-known undertaker, the first to consume an entire pumpkin with a salt-spoon being adjudged the winner), bob-apple, kiss-in-the-ring, catch-'em-alive-o (played in the Northumbrian way, with two packs of rubber cards and a set of fire-irons), sock-marrow and garden-scandal.

In the last-named game, the players simply form a circle and make rude remarks about one another's appearance, clothing, antecedents, morals, relatives and table-manners. This causes roars of laughter and may be continued until some hyper-sensitive player bursts into tears and has to go home in a cab. For sock-marrow—or vegetable-football, as it is called in Wessex—a real marrow is required; and as this is unlikely to survive the romp, the wise host will obtain

*Prevention of
Spiders*

one from a greengrocer rather than submit any of his own prize-winning specimens to so arduous an ordeal.

The English climate being what it is, garden-parties are very liable to be interrupted by sudden V-shaped or rectangular depressions from Iceland and elsewhere. When this occurs, the host must either allow his guests to shelter in the tool-shed until the storm has abated, or provide them with goloshes. On the other hand, guests who are stung by adders, savaged by goshawks, or otherwise injured during the revels, have no claim on him, such mishaps being regarded in the trade as temporarily occupational hazards. All the same, a really thoughtful host—and aren't we all?—will supply small inexpensive umbrellas, designed to be attached to the hat, for those of his guests who are naturally attractive to spiders.

As the mere rumour that a garden-party is being held at No. 17—or "The Larches", or "Sans Souci", or wherever it may be—is enough to bring every neighbour within eyeshot to an overlooking window, the best tea-service should always be used on these occasions, and at least one really imposing cake hired for the day to give the necessary tone to the festivities, because these things get about, and people talk so.

GARDEN ENTERTAINMENTS

As it happens, neither Mr. Heath Robinson nor I would attend any kind of garden-party unless we were paid handsomely to do so. Still, we realize that it takes all sorts to make a world, and these few simple wrinkles will, we trust, prove of service to those who are never so happy as when toying with stale seedcake and tepid tea in a powerful east wind and beneath a lowering sky.

Taking it all in all, that is pretty broad-minded and altruistic of us, we do think.

A Splint

The Bulbul Tree

TAILPIECE

In a book of this size, designed primarily to be worn in the hip-pocket as a protection against kicks in the coccyx, it is impossible to do more than scratch the surface of so vast a subject as horticulture. We have been unable, for example, to make any reference to the cultivation of yams and bulbul-trees—though this, in a way, is just as well, as a yam is one of the two things Mr. Heath Robinson is unable to draw (the other being a bulbul-tree).

The fact that neither Mr. Heath ("Towser") Robinson nor myself has ever grown any of the flowers or vegetables mentioned in this work will not, we hope, detract from its educational value or its usefulness as a fly-swatter. After all, very few dramatic critics—a curious breed of men, remarkable chiefly for their ability to sleep through the loudest shows—have ever written plays; and, of those who have, the majority are now wishing that they had chosen something easier, such as making little woollen models of the Albert Hall. The looker-on, in other words, sees most of the game; and as onlookers (preferably from arm-chairs, with

a large jug of something soothing within easy reach)
Mr. Heath Robinson and I acknowledge few superiors
below the rank of K.B.E.

Modest to the last, we do not claim that after
one quick perusal of this book anybody can rush out
and grow an orchid. In gardening, as in garrotting,
experientia docet (experience teaches), and the young
gardener must serve a long apprenticeship to Nature
and suffer many bitter disappointments before he can
back himself to grow even a daffodil at his first attempt.
But by following the common-sense rules hereinbefore
set forth (a phrase borrowed, on our note of hand alone,
from our solicitors, Messrs. Mundesley, Tewkesbury,
Wednesbury, Thursley, Filey, Saturday, and Sudbury,
to whom all inquiries re libel should be addressed) he
should in time be able to grow something sufficiently
floral to impress his relatives-by-marriage when they

The Looker-On Sees Most of the Game

To Impress His Relatives by Marriage

call—as relatives-by-marriage will—to raise their eyebrows at his furniture and commiserate with his wife.

It may be objected that, at the time of going to press, no mention has been made of the tools, implements and dinguses without which not even Contrary Mary could have made her garden grow. Well, between you and us, that is simply because nobody in the garden-implement business seems inclined to requite us for any such mention. Relenting slightly, however, I will refer briefly to certain by-products of Mr. Heath Robinson's fertile brain—"Old Faithful", as we call it lovingly—which are designed solely to ease the gardener's manual lot and can be constructed without much difficulty by anybody with a talent for such work.

These include the Combined Telescopic Spaderake, for those who long to dig and rake at the same time, the while humming an old sea-shanty; the Fork-Syringe, which is precisely what its name implies; the Twinspout Waterpot, for gardeners who wish to deluge their fuchsias, ferns and feet simultaneously by a simple

The Telescopic Spaderake

The Fork-Syringe

For Rolling Circular Paths

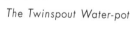

The Twinspout Water-pot

SOME USEFUL GARDEN APPLIANCES

The "Osoeezi" Slugsticker

sideways movement of the wrist; the "Inebriate" roller, for rolling unstraight garden-paths; and the "Osoeezi" Slugsticker, which—like an incompetent statesman— explains itself.

Other horticultural necessities, such as hoes, trowels, flower-pots, gumboots, Old Vegetarian blazers and jam-jars for the enticement of wasps, can either be bought of any reputable dealer or borrowed from anybody who seems disposed to lend them.

Naturally, Mr. Heath Robinson and I expect no gratitude or fan-mail in return for our efforts on behalf of Britain's gardening classes. What we have accomplished, such as it is, has been done with no hope of personal gain, but because we hold strong views

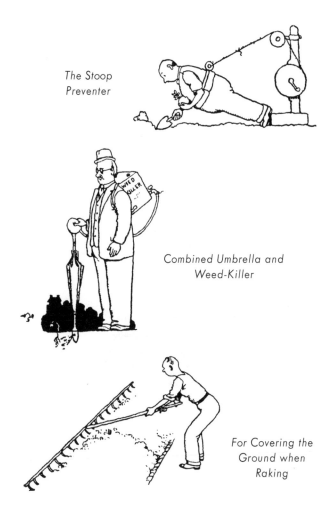

The Stoop Preventer

Combined Umbrella and Weed-Killer

For Covering the Ground when Raking

MORE USEFUL APPLIANCES

concerning our duty to mankind (and that includes even *you*, sir, with the drop-curtain moustache and the blood-orange). Gifts of flowers, raspberries, small sums of money, etc., will, however, be accepted in the spirit in which they are offered. As these, if sent to us c/o the publishers, will probably never reach us, they should be despatched, carriage paid, to our respective private addresses.

And there, I think, we will let the matter rest.

THE END

Shelter

Disposing of Local Rainfall